I am an ARO PUBLISHING THIRTY WORD BOOK
My thirty words are:

a	have	soup
am	I	take
and	knees	some
are	lip	talk
best	my	to
cold	nose	toes
drip	rest	told
feel(ing)	shaky	wheeze
from	sneeze	whiff
froze	sniff	with

MY FIRST THIRTY WORD BOOKS

My First Cold

Story by Julia Allen
Pictures by Bob Reese

 ARO PUBLISHING

My toes and nose

are feeling froze.

I feel a wheeze

and then I sneeze.

Drip, drip,

from nose to lip.

I have a talk

with my Doc.

I am told

I have a cold.

I feel a droop.

I have some soup!

I have a sniff.

I take a whiff.

I sneeze

and sneeze.

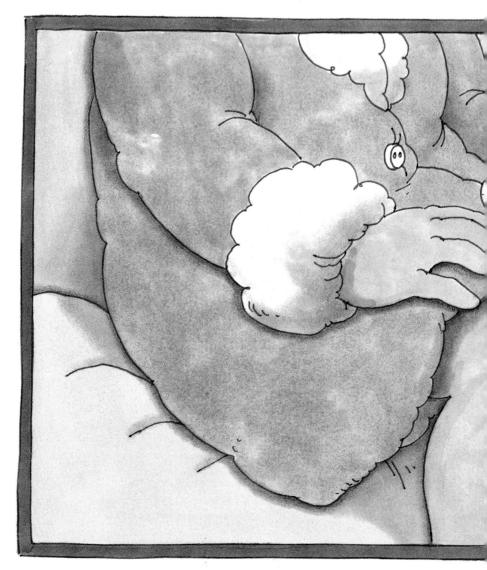

I have

shaky knees.

I have some rest,

I feel my best!